For River & Henry
...and Johnny, of course.

I0559122

Meet Johnny Ringtail (2nd Edition)
Jason Manning
ISBN: 979-8-9912677-0-0 (paperback) 979-8-9912677-1-7 (hardcover)

There once was a young cat who lived in our neighborhood.

He did not have a home.

But he did have a long, long tail with brown and white rings.

Is someone talking about me?

How many rings can you count?

The cat with the rings on his tail came to our porch one day.

He laid down and looked at us.

He wanted to be fed.

He wanted to be petted.

We fed him and petted him. Then we let him come inside.

He laid down on our couch. It was very comfortable.

The cat decided to stay with us.

We named him Johnny Ringtail, because of his long tail with the brown and white rings.

He really liked the couch.

How many rings can you count?

Cats like to relax.

Sometimes Johnny lays on the floor.

Is he waiting for something?

Cats are very clean. They clean their fur with their tongue.

Their tongues are rough and scratchy, like sandpaper. It makes them good for cleaning fur.

To reach every spot Johnny Ringtail has to bend into strange positions.

Doesn't he look funny?

Slurp!

Slurp!

Slurp!

Cats like small, cozy spaces.
It makes them feel safe.
Johnny likes to sit in empty boxes.

Can you still see me?

How many rings can you count?

Sometimes Johnny gets into things he shouldn't. Once he fell asleep in a suitcase before we could unpack it.

Another time he sat in the planter and smooshed the lettuce.

Johnny Ringtail eats and sleeps indoors. But he spends most of his day outside.

It's good to have land.

Sometimes Johnny climbs the big silver maple tree in the back yard.

He thinks no one can see him when he hides there.

I've been spotted!

I own the night!

Now how do I get down?

One night he even climbed onto the roof of the neighbor's garage. It was fun at first....
but then he couldn't get down again!
We needed a ladder to help him.

Goldfinch

Nuthatch

Blue Jay

Many birds come to the feeder in our back yard.

Can you name the different kinds?

Cardinal

Cats are hunters. Johnny tries to hunt the birds.

Why aren't the birds coming?

Luckily for them, he's not very good at it.

There are many other cats in the neighborhood. Some of them gather on the porch across the street.

We like to watch them and give them names.

Holstein

Tuxedo Cat

Fat John

Black Tom

Fat Ginger

Mustache Cat

Alice

Tortisha

Tabby Hayes

Wulfida

Sometimes cats fight one another. Male cats are called "toms." Tomcats often fight.

But sometimes cats get along. Johnny Ringtail is friends with Shaggy Larry.

They sit together in the driveway.

Look how long that ringtail is!

How many rings can you count?

When winter comes, Johnny stays inside more. But sometimes he goes out to play in the snow.

Now I can blend in!

At Christmas time, Johnny loves sleeping under the tree.

One March, Johnny Ringtail was happy to smell spring in the air.

What he didn't know was that it was time for us to move to a new house.

Cats do not like change.

Johnny did not want to go.

After we moved, Johnny was very sad.

He missed the old house.

He missed the old yard.

He missed the big maple tree.

He missed the other cats.

This new place was strange.

He was scared to go outside.

He just looked out the window and cried.

Johnny had to be brave.

After a few days, he went out to explore the new yard.

This isn't so bad

It wasn't so scary once he got used to it.

There were new places to sit and keep watch.

There are still birds at the feeder.
And new animals like wild turkey and deer.

Call me Johnny Walks-With-Deer

It took a little while...

But now Johnny Ringtail is happy in his new home.